YOU CAN'T STOP SOPHIE NOW!

YOU CAN'T STOP SOPHIE NOW!

SARAH FISCHER POINTER
Vanessa Alexandre

Mascot Books

This book is for my wonderful parents, Dave and Sue, who always taught me to reach for the stars. And for my loving husband, whose love strengthens me every day. Also dedicated to the fantastic staff and volunteers at Blaze Sports and the Rockford Park District, without whom "Sophie" would never have discovered her fighting spirit.

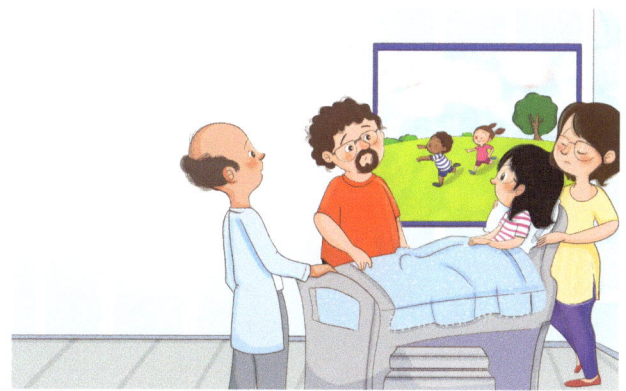

Sophie Swanson looked out the hospital window at the kids running around outside. "Can I please get up and play with them?" she begged her father.

"I'm afraid not, my girl," he answered with tears in his eyes.

Sophie sighed. While she understood why she couldn't get out of her hospital bed and play, she still didn't like it. When her doctor had seen Sophie two days after her surgery, he brought a pointy silver instrument with him. "Now, I'm going to poke your legs with this," he explained, "and i want you to tell me when you can feel it, okay?"

Sophie nodded, and the doctor nudged her big toe. "Can you feel this?" She shook her head quietly. Her legs felt numb, as if they had gone to sleep.

The doctor prodded her ankle, then her knee, asking if she could feel it each time, and each time she shook her head. Finally, he poked her in the stomach and she cried "I can feel that!"

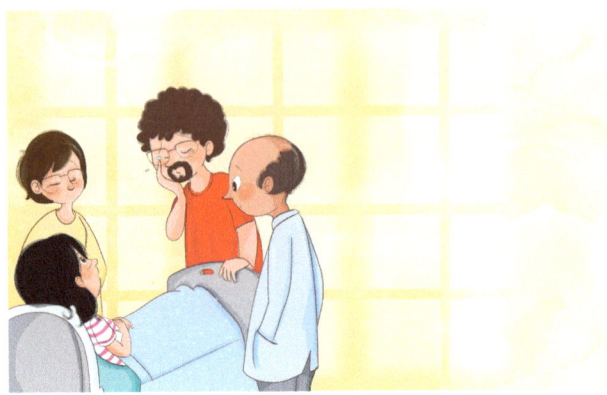

The doctor put his silver instrument away. "Sophie, I told your parents that we hadn't seen your legs move since the surgery. We were hoping that, maybe, given a little time, they would move again. Can you move your legs at all for me?"

She stared at her legs and told them to move, but nothing happened. "They won't move," she muttered.

The doctor nodded quietly and put his hand on hers. "I have some bad news for you, Sophie. It's been a few days since your surgery now, and if the feeling and movement in your legs hasn't come back yet, it's unlikely that they ever will."

"You mean, I'll never be able to walk again?" she squeaked.

He his head slowly. "At this point, the paralysis may be permanent. We should probably start discussing physical therapy, and a wheelchair for mobility. I'm so sorry."

Her mom started to cry, and her dad turned his head away to hide his tears. Even though Sophie was still in shock, she felt like she needed to comfort them.

Sophie squeezed her father's hand and said," Don't be sad, Daddy. I'm not sad." Her father gave her a tearful smile.

After that, Sophie threw everything she had into her therapy. She was determined to walk. But four months late,r Sophie still couldn't feel or move her legs. The doctors said there was nothing more they could do for her and sent her home with a wheelchair. She would have to continue physical therapy once a week to stretch her legs, but all the doctors and therapists agreed that she would not walk again.

Sophie tried to put on a brave face for her parents because she could see that they were hurting, but when school started up again in August, Sophie started to feel very sad. Before her surgery, she had loved to run and play with her friends at recess and had even played basketball in a local kids' league at the YMCA. Now, though, Sophie felt like she couldn't do anything without someone helping her.

Seeing other kids run around the playground reminded Sophie that she would never run again. Hearing her friends talk about basketball practice made Sophie sad because she was afraid she would never play her favorite sport again. She stopped going to practice and stayed in her classroom during recess.

One Saturday morning in early September, Sophie was at the mall with her parents. Her mother was pushing Sophie's wheelchair through a department store while her father shopped for tools. Sophie heard a lot of noise and noticed a large crowd outside the store. Feeling curious, she pushed herself out to the lobby. Two basketball hoops had been set up, and on the court was the most amazing thing Sophie had ever seen: people in wheelchairs playing basketball!

All of the players were in wheelchairs, like Sophie, but they weren't letting that stop them from playing basketball. Not only were they playing basketball, they were playing even faster and better than walking players Sophie had seen. She couldn't tear her eyes away from the game, and once it was over she tugged on her mother's sweater and asked, "Can I play?"

Her mother pushed Sophie's chair up to one of the players. "Hello! My name is Susanna, and this is my daughter, Sophie. She's always loved basketball. Do you all play for a team?"

The man smiled at Sophie. "Nice to meet you both, I'm Junior. We play for a team called the Rockford Chariots. Have you ever seen wheelchair basketball before?"

"No, but it looks so cool!" Sophie exclaimed. "Is it only for adults?"

Junior laughed. "No, there are teams for kids, too. Here in Rockford, we have the Jr. Chariots. Let me give you one of their fliers. It has the dates, times and addresses of their practices and games this season. I know they'd love to have another player."

Sophie's mother took the flier and thanked the man before going back into the store with Sophie and her father. "Can I really join the team?" Sophie asked her parents.

Her father looked at the flier and said "Well, it looks like they practice on Tuesday nights at a high school here in Rockford. Practices start next week. We could make that work."

"I wish practice was tomorrow, not next week!" Sophie exclaimed.

"Tuesday will be here before you know it," her father said with a laugh, ruffling Sophie's hair.

"I sure hope so!" she said.

Sophie suddenly couldn't wait for school the next day. She was going to tell her friends all about what she'd seen at the mall and about the new team she was going to play on. Even if she could never walk again, maybe she could play basketball again. Just a different kind of basketball.

As her mother drove her to her first practice, Sophie felt very nervous. She hadn't tried to dribble or pass a ball since her surgery. When she pushed herself into the high school, she heard basketballs pounding on the floor, kids talking and laughing, and wheels squealing. The original basketball hoops were locked in place against the ceiling. In their place, at each end of the court were lower basketball hoops on wheels.

Sophie saw some kids in wheelchairs dribbling and passing basketballs to each other, along with some parents sitting in bleachers along the wall. One of the kids out on the basketball court was a girl, but the rest of them were boys. The girl had long brown hair and had both of her legs missing below the knee. Some of the boys also had a part of a leg or even a whole leg missing, but a few of them had very skinny legs like Sophie. She wondered if they were paralyzed like she was.

The girl noticed Sophie and came over. "Hi, I'm Ginny," she said, smiling and putting out her hand. "You must be new?"

"Yeah, I'm Sophie." She shook the girl's hand shyly and noticed that she didn't look much older than Sophie was.

"Nice to meet you, Sophie. I think you'll like playing with us." She led Sophie over to the group in the middle of the gym and introduced her to the coaches and a few of the kids. The head coach, Tom, was a short African AMerican man with a big, friendly smile. He shook Sophie's hand and welcomed her to the team.

Sophie pointed at the basketball hoops. "Whey are these hoops lower than the others? I saw some people playing wheelchair basketball last weekend, and they were playing with taller hoops."

"Oh," Ginny said, "You must have seen the adult team. They play with regular hoops that are ten feet high. Junior teams play with hoops that are eight and a half feet high. You don't get to ten foot hoops until you get into junior high or high school."

Tom called the team together. "I'd like to introduce everyone to Sophie! She's here to join our team, and I hope you'll all give her a warm welcome." Everyone clapped while Sophie blushed. "So, let's start this practice off with some laps! I want ten laps around the gym." He blew his whistle and the kids took off, wanting to the first to finish.

After they were warmed up, Tom said "Next, let's practice our ball handling. In wheelchair basketball, you can only push your wheelchair twice before you have to dribble. I want everyone to split up into groups of three and take turns dribbling up and down the court."

Ginny asked Sophie and a boy named Aaron, who had cerebral palsy, to be in a group with her. Both of them had been on the team for a year already. When Ginny took the first turn dribbling the ball, it looked like she was floating on cloud. She took two pushes of her chair and dribbled the ball with her right hand. Push, push, dribble. Then she took two more pushes and dribbled the ball with her left hand. Push, push, dribble. Sophie was very impressed.

When she got back to the starting line, Ginny passed Aaron the ball and he sped off down the court. Push, push, dribble. Next, he put the ball in his lap, took one push of his chair, and dribbled with his left hand. Push, dribble. He was going even faster than Ginny had. By the time he got back to the starting line, she was feeling sick to her stomach.

Aaron tossed the ball right into her lap and Sophie caught it. She pushed her chair forward. Push, push, push.

"Don't forget, you can only touch your wheels two times before you have to dribble the ball," Ginny called.

"Oh, no! I forgot!" Sophie said nervously. She pushed herself once, leaned forward, and dribbled the ball straight down. The ball hit her foot and bounced off, which sent it flying across the gym. Sophie rushed after the ball, grabbed it quickly, and put it back in her lap. She went back to the starting line and tried again. This time, when she dribbled it, the ball bounced off her wheel and rolled back to the starting line. Sophie hung her head, feeling embarrassed.

Aaron saw how hard Sophie was trying and passed the ball back to her. "Try not dribbling the ball straight down. If you dribble it straight down, it's going to bounce off or your chair. But if you dribble a little further out, you won't hit anything."

Sophie smiled back and put the ball in her lap. She took two pushes down the court, stopped her chair, took the ball in her right hand, and dribbled it a couple feet to her right, away from her wheel. This time, the ball bounced and came back to her hand. Smiling widely, Sophie took two more pushes, stopped her chair, and dribbled once with her right hand. Push. Push. Stop. Dribble. She did this a few more time until she made it back to the starting line.

Ginny and Aaron gave her high fives. "Good job!" Aaron said. "You don't always want to stop to dribble, though, because that gives someone the chance to catch up to you and grab the ball."

"You're right. I didn't think about that," Sophie realized.

Tom called the team together and said "Well done, everyone! That's all the time we have for today, but keep on practicing and we'll see you next week."

When Sophie and her parents arrived at the first game of the season, the coaches and kids all greeted her happily. She saw that a lot of her teammates were already warming up; doing laps, passing balls to each other, or shooting hoops. Sophie decided to practice her dribbling a little more before the game. She grabbed a ball off the rack and started pushing. Push, push, dribble.

Sophie decided to try and dribble with her left hand this time. She gave two pushes of her wheelchair and tried dribbling once, away from her left wheel. Push, push, dribble. The ball came bouncing right back to her. "Yes!" Sophie said.

Soon, it was time for the game to start. Tom called the team together and gave them a short pep talk. He told Sophie to wait on the bench, but about ten minutes in, Tom called her to his side. "I want you to go in," he said.

"What?!" Sophie squeaked, suddenly feeling nervous.

"I want you to go in for Ginny, she needs a break," Tom said.

"But it's my first game!" Sophie muttered.

Tom put a reassuring hand on her shoulder and said, "Don't worry. I have faith in you. You can do this!"

Ginny came over to the bench, sweaty and out of breath, and gave Sophie a high five as she headed onto the court. Four boys were out on the court for the Jr. Chariots: Aaron, Carson, Nelson and Bart. Aaron was on the sidelines near the Jr. Warriors bench, ready to pass the ball in. The referee blew his whistle and Aaron passed the ball to Nelson. All three boys headed towards their basket.

Nelson got stopped by a Jr. Warriors player, saw that Sophie was open, and passed the ball to her. Sophie's heart was pounding so hard it felt like it would come right out of her chest. She gave two big pushes of her chair. Without stopping or touching her wheels, she took the ball in her right hand and dribbled it. It bounced back to her hand!

Sophie put the ball in her lap and gave another big push towards the Jr. Chariots basket. Bart was right underneath the basket and had nobody guarding him, so she called his name and tossed him the ball.

Bart caught it with both hands and took the shot. *Swoosh!* The ball went sailing through the net!

Sophie couldn't get the smile off her face for the rest of the day. She realized that what her mother had said was true. You can do anything you put your mind to, even if you have to do it a little differently. And if being in a wheelchair couldn't stop Sophie from playing her favorite sport, she wasn't going to let anything stop her from reaching for her dreams.

 Sarah Fischer Pointer is a licensed attorney in Florida and enjoys writing children's books in her free time. Originally from Dixon, Illinois, she currently lives in Southwest Florida with her husband and their two cats. Her favorite sport is wheelchair basketball, which she played from 1996- 2005 through the Blaze Sports Foundation and the Rockford Park District. Although she no longer plays basketball, she still enjoys watching it and will always consider herself a Rockford Chariot.

www.ingramcontent.com/pod-product-compliance
Lightning Source LLC
LaVergne TN
LVHW071701060526
838201LV00037B/397